TRUE STORIES

CAROLIENA CABADA

Thank you for reading
this book!

From Iowa, U.S.A.

Caroliene C

For information contact:

Unsolicited Press

Portland, Oregon

www.unsolicitedpress.com

orders@unsolicitedpress.com

619-354-8005

Cover Design: Kathryn Gerhardt

Editor: Summer Stewart

ISBN: 978-1-963115-03-1

POEMS

100-Year Storm

Part I Tropical Disturbance: Thunderstorms with light cyclonic circulation

Part II Tropical Depression: Wind speeds between 20 and 34 knots (23–39 mph)

For Aaron: first.

100-Year Storm

or a storm of a magnitude that has a 1-in-100 chance of occurring any
        given year,
or the two times in as many decades my hometown has severely flooded,
or a hurricane that was not meant to hit Manhattan that hard,
or typhoons so nice they're named twice,
or those same typhoon names removed from a list,
or a sure sign of the apocalypse,
or a storm that changes the scale by which we measure,
or another name, retired,
or what catches us all unaware,
or everything we should have seen coming if we stayed vigilant,
or ancestral ghosts haunting us,
or all the heat and pressure in the atmosphere has to go somewhere,
or hurricane-force winds on the Great Plains,
or what fells the old-growth walnut by the brook,
or the stress that's built inside me since birth,
or anger never given a vent,
or the whistle of the worst teakettle,
or a list of the deceased,
or the newsfeed scroll of the safe,
or names of everyone you wish you left behind,
or what goes around comes around and around and around,
or the aftermath of a burn,
or where I go when I need to be alone,
or a cyclops wandering the earth,

or a storm of a magnitude that is more likely to happen now: last year, this year, and every year to come.

PART I

TROPICAL DISTURBANCE: THUNDERSTORMS WITH LIGHT CYCLONIC CIRCULATION

Out of Season

Snow fell before leaves did
from bent maple branches.
Shadows stretched at ten
in the morning. Frost melted
where dawn slid through
the sides of the bridge, remained
slick in the railing's shade.
Burnished bronze flakes fluttered
down from a black oak, fire
on patchy, white down.
The afternoon washed it all
with a raindrop song dripping
from an umbrella dome.
Shadows grew tall
in the evening, light peeking
through clouds, feet
sinking heels-first in the lawn.

Romantic Aubade

I wake up
  early with you as
sunrise lights the glass
  on westward buildings.

The coffeemaker presses
  our eyelids open,
soft in the glow
  of winter light.

There is a wrong way
  to wake a part of you,
hibernating tilted
  away from the sun,

And there are so many
  right ways to rouse you
from slumber. Trust me,
  I'm remembering them all.

Feeding Friends

We are never getting married, and yet
this home is like Bethsaida: shortage
at first. Worry in a lean season, sage
flavoring everything soft green. We get
fuller with time, with five loaves and two fish.
We grow, breaking bread with friends, make it work
because we are hungry. Now, we can lurk
in the holiest places. Yes, a dish
can multiply. There is magic in this
shared meal. Humble, we bow our heads with grace.
We say no prayer, but here we make a place
at the table, are prolific in bliss.
We are never getting married, but my
love is Cana, transfiguring this wine.

Is it nice where you are?

Here there is sunlight on the dewdrops,
glistening the leaves. Glitter hints
the snap peas they'll grow into
end of spring. The wood porch
is warm, and the seat a dream nap
stretched out in a field.
Unnamed birds
wing their way, and sing
in the branches of an old fir.
There is nothing like it. Feast
for every sense. In the evenings,
all there is, is rest. Is it nice,
where you are? Though I may pace
the same carpeted square feet, lushness
blooms from my vacuum tracks.
Is it nice? Tell me,
it is nice where you are?

On a Bad Day

I toss the blankets off my legs. Despair
isn't a good look on anyone. Air
fresh feels cool on skin, but the smell of my
downward spiral is onion powder. Try
falling asleep to the smell of wasted
potential. The grandfather clocks had ticked
much faster today, my spinning tighter
on thin ice, the kind that's frozen so clear
that it cracks into rainbows when you step,
become Jesus on water. Hoarders kept
all the beauty of unanswered questions.
I cry because my every intention
to be good gets smothered by my rank dread.
When I wake, my dreams melt inside my head.

Waking Up During a Storm

East wind changes. Lightning illuminates
the bedroom wall. Thunder smacks skin, rumbles
soothing after. Night passes, at this rate
sieves through eyelids, gone with the gentle grumbles
of an empty stomach. This, too, shall pass.
With sunrise comes shadows and graying light
thinned by tiny water drops gaining mass
into another thunderhead. It might
break on this great plain, or travel on wind
to the mountain. But days will be long dark,
sunshine found in cups, robins determined
to out-sing the gloom. A calendar mark
to remember another day is gone.
The year passes and always feels so long.

New Passover

Mark this house as salvation
for the storm-blown and savage.

Wind whistles through a crack
around the glass, but the view

bursts green, gold. Open the doors
to the hard times. Invite

the down-on-their-luck. Feed them
all that you have, and make more

from the scraps. As long as
everyone, even God, takes half, we'll

never reach zero. Lightning
strikes a block away.

If there are victims, they
may not have been wicked.

Maybe they just settled in
for another night of distance.

Stay in. Venture out only
to be of assistance.

Aubade, Inside

light brightens horizon,
dissolves darkness

sunrise reaches the bed
we've slept in,
smooth again for dozing
afternoon on top of covers

of course we are lovers

we hold each other's worries in
our stomachs, feed them
with every bite of news
scrolling our screens

in this life there are beds
and there are beds

listen, birdsong
heralds springtime

flowered trees
lose blossoms in the hail, but still
we're awe-struck, transfixed,
blink the storms away,

rub eyes, stare sunlight,
tomorrow do it over again.

What Grows in the Garden

We both stay awake all night
trying to make it through a trial.
Pluck a spearmint leaf to rest on
a tongue like the body
of a savior, savor sweet green
and blue-tint flavor. Sharp cool
keeps one of us awake.
Fresh figs split open, reveal
slick insides. Eat just enough
to stave off slumber, stay
hungry. What else to sink
our teeth into to keep us going
until fluorescent dawn? You
sip the cold water, and my eyes
droop from the wine.

I don't want to die

for anything I
don't think would die for
me. I don't want to
die for anything I did
not ask to die
for me. I don't want
to die for anything
that's just to die for.
I don't want to die   I
don't want to die   I don't
want to die   I don't want
to die   I don't want to
die   I don't

23

PART II

TROPICAL DEPRESSION:
WIND SPEEDS BETWEEN 20 AND 34 KNOTS
(23-39 MPH)

Urgent Care

Right now, to heal is   to sit

at home with your fears.   To hold them

in your mind,   your joys.

Celebrate everything.   For now, we listen

to the news   in other states.

Iowa has not   sheltered in place.

It is urgent to   not go anywhere.

Thank your god for   sparing you

so far.   Take your   destiny into your

own hands by   control, wash them,

washing everything,   spare delivery.

Who's not taking   any chances? Not only

you.   Not only me.

Hard Times

We're afraid we don't have much
        to offer. On a normal day, we'd give
away the contents of our pantry,
        mixed and baked into decadent delight.

Right now, all we have to give
        are the first salmon we came across.
It's bad luck to fish so early, worse
        to give it away like it's ours

and not the river's. We're afraid
        of so much, most of which we'll
keep behind closed lips while we
        chew, politely. We're afraid

we're not even the best company,
        left too long our insecurities
became feral. All we have
        to give is all we have.

It's not much, we're afraid.
        On a normal day, we could raise
your spirits in a toast. On a normal
        day, we could make you laugh.
We're sorry. We don't feel much

like laughing when we fear
the brook drying up. We don't know
how to open our mouths and not ask

how you are doing, how you
are holding up, how you are finding
your days when the heat seems
to smother your cool.

We don't know how to not ask,
"Are you afraid, too?" How soon
is too soon to get existential,
to talk about rational fears?

We're afraid we don't have much.
We're afraid we don't have enough.
We're not afraid of what happens
when we give our one fish

to a hungry man. We're not
afraid of a flood. We're not afraid
of bad luck. We just want
what we've always shared.

Staying In

Resilience has a limit. To stay
sequestered for long, invites indifference.
After this, there is no after. You pray
for this to pass. Stay inside this instant.
There's a wind blowing hard enough to twist
every sentence to doubt. Who knows what's right?
What harm comes from believing in this
crowned virus as monarch? The way we fight
is by bed rest, comfort, home remedy
if you're privileged. No salvation if not.
Your canceled milestone is a tragedy.
But your favorite god or goddess has caught
their destiny. After this, there is no
after, only one direction to go.

On the First Nice Day

On the first nice day of the summer
I wrote a sad poem. The air
quality index was in the green,
and I was cool in the shade.
Cool enough that sweat didn't bead
slick behind my knees, or where my
thighs slid together.
Dry, I wrote a sad poem about time
melting and running
freely. It won't be
the only poem I write.
That page wasn't big enough
for every metaphor I ever want to use.
On the first nice day
of the summer, I wrote a sad poem
because it was the first
clear day—air quality index
low and in the green—
where I could breathe that needed
sigh of relief. Lately
I've been afraid to exhale too hard.
Nowadays, the sun sets, burnt crisp
at its circular edge. My sadness
couldn't hold a candle.
I might have ruined

the first nice day—air quality
index in the green—with my
paltry feelings.

I have been burying

my toes under covers, under

                       warmth when cold air

        through the window

is the   closest

                   to outside I can get.

       Let's stay in   bed

longer than the hours

             we have in   a day,

       longer than we can guarantee.

Sing to me about   cherries

           with the pit in the middle.

       Tell me about what's sweet,

though the heart of   it

           cracks teeth.

By the time this reaches you

the headlines will have changed, new
words schooling, hooking eyes
like fishing wire, spinners
made to look like dinner sparkling
on the surface. By the time this
reaches you, you might be
moved to a new place, setting up
camp, living out a dream. Where
do you think you're going? Asking
feels like an answer.
By the time this reaches
you, I'll be somewhere else,
too, making some new world
to climb in and hide. We'll meet again
one day. We'll meet again one day.

How to Fill a Void

After will happen in slow motion.
Every action heightened, sanguine
emotion blushing skin on necks
and chests. Heads rest on shoulders
squared and solid from the march.
Complex distance. Want
and not want. After, days will be
sharper, more nerves and blood
vessels at the surface, all vital.
Nothing will be empty—nature
abhors a vacuum. How to fill
a void, how to jump across a gap,
synapse, electricity. After, after,
after, we yearn for the conclusion,
seek closure—sleep through it.

Sunset

At sunset the day cracked open
        Chest caved a bruised center
There used to be boulders
        settled grew moss to cover
fissure hairline jagged
        split on scraping surface
Been trying
        feeling sunlight
Sat in the patch
        wandering across carpet
gaze framed by eyelashes dazzling
        in metal light   The world
goes out with a bang
        Been cracking open
the light in everything so that it
        doesn't crack me

A Short Storm

In the Midwest, storms go as soon as they
arrive. Torrential downpour of water
in liquid form or ice. Everyone, stay
inside. This is not weather to dance. Turn
the lights off and observe the sun shower.
Clouds diffuse the glow and turn to static.
Witness the sky falling in past the hour,
weather mimicking moods, turns erratic.
Earth, maybe, is stir-crazy, too, wishes
for a spring of realignment, bringing
chaotic blossoming, and finishes
with a steady drip of robins singing.
Here, the sunset shines throughout the rainstorm,
gives thunder lurid color and its form.

Manhattan Stars

Abandoned Broadway. Singular figure walking wind-whipped
and swift. Storm coming. Glass-rattling violent clash,

water against windows. A yell when the power goes out.
I've seen worse, or I think I have. On the sixth floor, I'm safe

from rising water, but not from the day after, when
New York City still has no power. My body is fine, but my mind

craves something it will never see again: Dark Manhattan. The
stars, for once, above the Washington Square arch.

No garish smudge of Times Square light. Or maybe I
imagined it. Blotted those beams out. I go back to

that quiet New York City, count down the days to the next
time a storm imposes solitude. Head up and tread water.

PART III

TROPICAL STORM:
WIND SPEEDS BETWEEN 35 AND 64 KNOTS
(40-73 MPH)

Nocturne

But does the day really start
if I can't
get out of bed?
I haven't slept right for weeks.
Golden hour is the only time
I'll look at the world I was meant
to light. Everything is gorgeous
from an angle. Even a crash
is softer on the bias.
I'm tired of my duty.
The sky looks better dappled
in faraway stars, ripples of dust
in a dark beam, reverse
engineering. Maybe the daytime
is overrated. Maybe the night's
year is here. Maybe there's a word
for a god's somnolence, specifically.
In the end, the world forces
a turn.

Behind smudged glass, we sat

watching hawks and shadows.
Sunset lights the underside
of glide wingspan, golden.
To be hollow-boned,
feathered, flicker yellow,
swooping fast on gale winds
rattling human windows. Two birds, circling,
seeming to hover, flap
only to course correct, grow
closer, then further. We sat,
pointed fingers as they turned
around maple boughs that shed seeds
in the summer.
Here, hunger pivots
for a kill, and sunset paints glass
fingerprints redder still.

Today's

time and the to-do list. *Trim fingernails and*
dismantle capitalism. What's wrong with taking
this as the break we all deserve? Fingerprints
on non-touchscreen glass; pretend it's smooth
and skin-like. Cover mouth with washed hands,
whisper a wish on the first star out the window.
Even the ones blinking warnings to low-flying
planes. Tomorrow, the list might just be
Exist, exist, exist.

Lessons to Learn from Herbicide-Resistant Waterhemp

Resilience, not reaction. Frustrated farmers will think
resistance a bridge to burn when they get to it. Burning
bridges leaves no way off the island except swimming.

Commonly known as tall waterhemp, *Amanranthus
tuberculatus* is persistent in Iowa fields. Resilience,
not escalation, a quiet death and life giving from
generation to generation.

This is the benefit of paying attention. Write down
what —cide means to you.
Herbi-
Pesti-
Geno-

        means required resistance, with
        reaction, resilience.

Morning After

Gently exfoliating face wash,
toner on a cotton pad, moisturizer
of choice, light to medium
BB cream around the eyes to hide
tiredness, black eyeliner
to emphasize sharp
rage, resilience. Last night
was tropical depression.
This morning it's Miss Tropical
Storm to you. Become more
Hurricane shade of eye shadow, more
Force To Be Reckoned With.
Cover up
a bloodshot eye, ice
reducing red puffiness from an ugly cry.

Yolanda

There is no smile when people call me.
Everything puckered, bared teeth, a tongue
pressed against corrugated
      roofs of mouth houses:
           Yolanda.
But they smile when their teeth
are knocked out by me, the gaps
like windows to open air.

How could they still welcome me?
Say, "Take this hunk of flesh
carved from the roasted pig.
      The skin is crunchy.
           The skin is the best part."
Here is the best part:
I prefer the name given
to me by the people
      I have hurt
          the most.

Futile Denial

Weather app says snow
  in April, hour by
hour, waiting between
  all four seasons of
the Northern Hemisphere's
  year. Gray snow banks blur,
refuse to refuse
  joy dripping from leaves,
despite ruined plans
  for tree plantings, for
spring. To let that
  future, gray despair
forecast its shadow
  in reverse—to give
up like it's futile—
  is its own kind of
denial. Because
  who knows? Maybe this year
we'll be direct,
  a doe's gaze pre-flight.
This year we'll be frank
  freezer-burned brown grass.
We'll be melting snow,
  a fiercer feeling
than hope.

I become a hurricane

again because I loved,
too much, and used the same words
for loving. Always flooding.
And eroding. And rising. And
swirling. All my first times
felt like whirling. A wind filled
the bedsheet sail and glided me.
In the bed sense, drench
is a good thing. But the fecund
waters of my body frightened.
The hunger of my legs
turned instead into running,
a river overflowing. I was
always sore in the morning.
What better word to describe
these rains from clear skies,
and dawn was pink outside
the way it wasn't quite so inside me.
And for that, I'll always
feel closed. This eye,
the bloody center, is a darker
texture. And yet, still salty
like tears or sea water.

The Last Word

Spiraling light draws
my eyes, seeing maple
seeds jamming
between balcony boards,
sails up, a mini fleet, fleeting.
The first summer storm smashed
through slats, debris
scattered on the porch below.
The downstairs neighbor
doesn't sweep.
Why should he? Turbulent
rainwater rivulets carry remnants
away. Seeds daydream a hundred years
dormant, then sprout to reclaim
the pavement. Imagine wordless
seeds having the final say.
Growing through concrete
statement. Tenacious root
sentence. All this in a seed.

Watershed

Foxconn sounds cartoonishly villainous. I am waiting
for the feel-good story. A girl writes a poem that saves
the Village of Gurnee, downstream. It would be that
easy. The poem would sound like a protest chant, and
its lines would look good on a poster. There would be
wordplay around the Wisconsin governor's name.

I have waited for the tidy conclusion. A girl's poem
saves the hometown she left. But lead has a way of
staying in the soil and getting into stems. It takes
forever to get rid of the traces. The poem quenches,
then

walks so another

protest poem could run, mimic

wild Des Plaines River.

PART IV

HURRICANE:
WIND SPEEDS GREATER THAN 64 KNOTS
(74 MPH)

I imagine turning to stare into the face

of the future   grasping
air between fingers   holding

not hands   they're slipping
wide eyes stinging   from staring

at a   distant   full   moon
you exist   you're right

in front of me   what chest burst
feeling   ripe pomegranate split skin

seeds inside   soft and sprouting
germinating   in its own   dissolving

flesh   that's the feeling
of the future   dusting

right   behind   me
I'll gasp and mourn   at the sight

Sandy, Scorned

New York hit me hard, so I hit back.
It said, "This hurts because I love you."
I said, "You better take that back." My
fingers bruised through Fifth Avenue and
roiled over Brooklyn. It said, "I know
I deserve this." I said, "You
deserve nothing." And my sisters longed
to protect me, longed for the crush of
concrete, longed to flip the money changers'
tables on Wall Street. But they could never
rise like me. They stayed equatorial,
kept hitting archipelagos. I
backhanded Manhattan and Long Island.
The winds changed. New York said, "I love you."
I gave it a black eye. I hit New
York. I saw an opportunity
and I took it.

How to Communicate Catastrophe

Give it a name. If you
name it, you own it: ask
Adam and the God he'd
chosen. Dominion is
another word for only.
Ask Eden. It was growing
wild just fine until
these humans
arrived. Give it back
its terrain: it will
mend, and still.
Give it a name—it will
take a body, too. Give it
an inch, it will blossom
for miles. In the end,
dominion sounds nicer
in a poem, and a naming
seems innocuous: that's
innocent. A name
can still strike fear,
retain its feeling, be
said wrong: make it right.

Pseudonymous

If I were brave enough, I would name myself Aphelion:
the point in the Earth's orbit where it is furthest from the
Sun. I invite you to read too much into it, believe that I
am saying I am at my furthest from the Son, and His
Father, and the ugly duckling that is the Holy Ghost.
Break down the etymology: "helios" as in "Sun" and
"apo" as in "away from," or else "apó" as in "grandchild"
in Tagalog. What a coincidence: I am far from the Sun
but still its grandchild.

Choosing names
is the first act of
creating.

I've Bitten Off More Than I Can Chew

I spit it
out, grab a knife
and fork,
slice this ridiculous
bespoke craft burger
into half-inch pieces
to re-savor.
So what if it's gross?
I do my best
before a meal.
Words are hungrier,
mouthful and thirsty.
Charred bell pepper,
klaxon red
burning redder,
feeding what fevers—
save scraps for later.
I do my best in
the kitchen,
chomped down
because hunger
made me.
Taste heat and
texture. Relish the sting.
Pick up tomorrow

where I left off,
reheat what I have.
Then fill me up
with what I wanted
so much
I was willing
to gag myself to get it.

More the Merrier

after Vern Rutsala

We do not answer the invitation.
Such a table laden with delicacies
arouses suspicion. Our bellies rumble.
We do not trust what is freely given.
We get by in the dust by virtue of
a virtuous neighbor. After each bite
of an apple, we pass it on. In this
way, we are full. When the call comes again,
we see a way to dull our sharp edges,
buff our surfaces until we could shine
and shatter like glass. In the end, the only
glitter that matters is water. Outside,
dust turns to mud, turns to soil we could sow
with seeds. Music plays from inside the feast
room. We eat figs and save leaves. On the third
call, we arrive and center our fruit on
the table. We come as we are, and sing.

Windfall

I've seen men ignore
figs in front of them, reach
for unripe greens holding fast to limbs
instead of fruit crush-flushed
and wind-fallen.
I waited
with grass-stained knees
for a turn around the garden,
tree of knowledge orchard.
Eating what was given, I learned
the sweetest juice came
from bruises on fruit
left by gravity
and the ground.
I know now
the first step of falling
in love is falling from grace.
Is picking figs
off the ground
for the banquet table
while having one
in your teeth
for a taste.

How to Be a Mystery

Animal tracks on the ream of snow
cover the frozen creek, swerving
away from the bank and back again.
Sometimes they
full stop in the middle.
That's when I wonder
and worry.

No scratchy signs of
scrabbling, fighting off something swooping
to lift with a razor grasp.
Just prints in a parallelogram,
describing their four-legged gait.
No smear of snow showing their body
dragging, falling, pulling away.

If they retraced their path
unerringly, placing feet exactly where they'd
been before, I need them to teach me
how to be a mystery.
And I need to tell them:
Retracing steps is not the same as
taking them back.

Getting Back to Being Myself Again

Shower water hits different after
a crying stint. It gets under my skin,
puckers it, reminds me that every
cell is thirsting. Hair
frizzes as it air-dries, shines
on the hundredth pass-through
with a smoothing comb. The mirror
says *Hallelujah, a human.* The human,
Hallelujah, some clean.
At night, the mattress
hits my hips different,
cradles my bones apart
as they sink into semi-firm
surfaces. Sleep comes
easier, sometimes. My bed
says, *Peace be with you,* and
my spine says, *And also*
with you. In the morning,
my feet hit the floor
different, settling
into arches as I stretch
and tremble my skeleton, breathe
like I mean it. How to make
a home in discomfort:
float on your back
and breathe deep.

Deliberately

Yesterday, I remarked on a maple
tree's buds visible through the window. My
friend knows what questions to ask to find out
what tree is about to bloom. I'll learn this
in time. I have plans to read the section
of the library dedicated to
Iowa wildlife. I've already learned
about sycamores' exfoliating
bark, described as "handsome" by botanists
for the cream-colored contrast against
dark leafless trees. I've learned so much.
Most of it by accident.
My friend used to scold me: "What could you learn
deliberately? Imagine where you would be."
But that has always been my problem. I imagine
so much I never wake up. This morning
I saw a walnut tree in shadow. Ten
hours from now it will be drip-dyed in gold.
And my friend will open soft flesh around
the wrinkled, hard shell of a wind-fallen fruit,
crack it open to get at the meat. I
won't yet know its blossoms or branches.

PART V

THE EYE

Emerging

Hungrier for birdsong, the soft melody
is the best thing I've ever tasted. Breakfast
warms the stomach—all else is air. And for me,
I imagine air will be enough to last
after a year of inside melancholy.
It was all still sweet. It was all a fast
lie to say I was fine. I know not to
keep secrets. Still, I close my mouth when I chew.

It's only polite to hide behind closed lips.
One day, I'll be a bird with my beak open
to deliver a call that echoes, cantrips
pushed through my throat. Morning is a spell that then
becomes a curse. I'll take coffee, cold, in sips
small enough to slide past the lump there. And when
it's time to navigate familiar
places, I'll know exactly where we are.

First, ask

How to start over: first ask forgiveness
of the places you raged in. Cleanliness
is close to godliness, but destruction
discriminates. You know this. That friction
creates heat, and someone cleans up the mess.

That someone is always one who has less.
Less money, less power, less loneliness.
That last is a somewhat happy notion—
if they didn't have to start over.

Fresh starts are not always empty. Distress
hollows hearts to float on a flood's egress
past a barrier, towards endless ocean.
Fill it up with apologies, diction
higher than helium, one last confess.
How to start over: first, ask.

A Final Supper

If the summer blaze persists until my
Judgment Day, I won't pray for another
winter. I'll spread my body out on fry
pan cast iron, then roll to the other
side and cook even. Already golden,
the skin can still be browner, more toothsome.
I hunger for char and am emboldened
to hold my barbecue for a ransom.
No one should feast on my body but me.
I shouldn't sacrifice my first life for
nonbelievers. Forgiveness isn't free.
When given a taste, the greedy ask more
of me. With hope, I try to rescue, yet
refusing, they sink in the watershed.

True Story

The river once flooded the K through 8
school in my hometown. When the waters took
weeks to recede, they held classes in the
town's only peach-colored outlet mall. Lunch
in the food court. Economics in a
house of commerce. Recess playing four-square
in the parking spaces painted white on
graying blacktop, dodging cars. But it won't
become a storied place. The town let the
mall fall apart, torn down for a Super
Wal-Mart where I once bought crusty bread and
salad greens with my dad on a health kick
and this was the cheapest produce in town.
I attended the new elementary
and middle built out the old school's kind
of red brick, Frank Lloyd Wright Prairie Style (it's
the Midwest) built further from the river
bed. In the sun-soaked nook of the middle
school library, I read a book written
about those kids in that mall during that
flood, going to school. I wonder: Next time
the waters rise, what incongruous place
will house our learning? The second amendment
in a Bass Pro Shop, hunting rifles on
the walls. Gladiators in a professional

football stadium after a hurricane.
Science experiments in a farm-to-table
restaurant. A while back, people just called
that home economics.

Aftermath

Gusts sucker punch,
                    steamroll,
          straighten gnarled
branches into wicked sharp
scratches at the screen door.
At best
          this is all.
          More often trees
stretch then fall into the door,
knocking so hard glass
                    shatters
          into every reckoning.
          What's with the tornado
warning? It's only a little
bit of wind. It's only a summer
          storm, gone
                    faster
than it came on, lingers
                    still
          in the power lines felled.
Every gust is a body slam.
                    Every
          slam is another day
left in the dark. The trees do
their part.

Inflorescence

The first summer after
       glaciers melted and dipped
the land, made it fertile,
       was still cool,
not yet heat, humidity,
       clear blue skies,
sweat in your eyes.

Soon, though, the sun at noon
       evaporated puddles, fed
milkweed, lead plant, big bluestem,
       coneflower, thistle, yarrow,
everything green
       that caresses and stings.

Turn your face to me.

Inflorescence, budding of flowers,
       is a poet's word now,
stripped of geometry
       as blossoms grow raucous
in oscillating seasons.

Sigh the scent of dust
        after a rain, washed out
atmosphere.

Now, spring is for lovers,
        and summer
is for lovers, too, dozing
        in the hottest time of day,
basking in the glow.

When the night sky clouds over,
        stars press their light through—
a surprise shooting star,
        wish at the ready.

Geo Logic

If glacier   then revelation

If sinking   then fen

If elevation   then atmosphere

If archive   then exclusivity

If narrow   then lauded

If salt   then solution

If melting   then violence

If time   then magnitude

If soft   then fossil

If immortal   then broken

If captured   then study

If open   then chipped

If observed   then waver

If hypothesis   then repetition

If carbon   then longevity

If oxygen   then rust

If burning   then prairie

If wildfire   then hunger

If feast   then greed

If potluck   then gift

If sugar   then humidity

If rain   then fulfillment

If lithic   then history

If month   then mourning

If water   then body

If touch   then home

If dreaming   then wake

Naming Conventions

The practice of naming (tropical cyclones):
>   easier to remember
>   easier   to report
>   short, distinctive
>   quicker and less subject to error

In the pursuit of a more organized and efficient naming system:
>   feminine names for storms
>   a list arranged alpabetically (sic)
>   male names for the Southern Hemisphere

1979:
>   men's names   alternate with the women's names
>   Six lists are used in rotation

if a storm is so deadly or costly   future use of its name   would be inappropriate

                    the offending name is stricken from the list and another name is selected to replace it:

>   Mangkhut (Philippines, 2018)
>   Irma and Maria (Caribbean, 2017)
>   Haiyan (Philippines, 2013)
>   Sandy (USA, 2012)
>   Katrina (USA, 2015)

Melting Cryosphere

Ice—cold solid and sharp—melts loud.
Imagine melting, compact stream
breaking: plunging berg, crashing
ice into ocean. Around me, I can't

imagine melting, compact stream,
constant shivering. Time turned
ice into ocean around me. I can't
deny how water breaks

constant shivering. Time turned
palms at poles into ice caps. I won't
deny how ice breaks
our belief, assume time changes

palms at poles into ice caps. I won't.
I only do what I can. For
disbelief, assume time will change.
Constant heat quietly deceives.

I only do what I can for
breaking, plunging berg, crashing.
Constant heat quietly deceives.
Ice—cold, solid, and sharp—melts loud.

Solastalgia

n. The feeling of homesickness without ever leaving home

Winter days half-melted,
compressed ripples,
dripped icicles
around this lake.
We haven't left here
for decades. We miss
it—this skating rink,
sled lane, no-man's-land
between snow forts.
Instead, shorelines
crumble. We do, too,
as muscle atrophies
from disuse,
as energy both
heats and cools. What
will come if we stay,
if this changes
before our eyes?
Water needs to run
downstream. It
might be time for
a new beginning, frozen
solid, even in a noon
sun. Clear ice

with light passing
through, bright enough
to beam us home, away.

NOTES AND ACKNOWLEDGMENTS

The stanza at the end of "Pseudonymous" is a line from Gina Apostol's Insurrecto (2018).

Text for "Naming Conventions" is from the World Meteorological Organization: https://public.wmo/int/en/About-us/FAQs/faqs-tropical-cyclones/tropical-cyclone-naming, Accessed 15 Nov 2019

Definition of solastalgia from "'Solastalgia': Arctic inhabitants overwhelmed by new form of climate grief" by Ossie Michelin, *The Guardian*, 15 Oct 2020, Accessed 15 Oct 2020. URL: https://www.theguardian.com/us-news/2020/oct/15/arctic-solastalgia-climate-crisis-inuit-indigenous

Information on sycamores in "Deliberately" from Clemson Cooperative Extension Home & Garden Information Center, published 1 Jun 1999, Accessed 13 Dec 2022. URL: https://hgic.clemson.edu/factsheet/sycamore/

Versions of the following poems have been published previously:

"100-Year Storm" in *The Babel Tower Notice Board*

"Is it nice where you are" and "Staying in" (published as "Sonnet Staying In") in *Verse-Virtual*

"Aubade, inside," "How to communicate catastrophe," "A short storm" (published as "Sonnet With A Short Storm"), "Aftermath," and "Waking up during a storm" (published as "Sonnet Waking Up During A Storm") in *Unpublishable Zine*

"What grows in the garden" in *Whale Road Review*

"I have been burying" published in *Across the Social Distances*

"Behind smudged glass, we sat" in *Front Porch Review*

"Today's" (published as Untitled) in *Backchannels Journal*

"Lessons to learn from herbicide-resistant waterhemp" and "New Passover" in *Lumiere* x *Elysian*'s Special Issue: Advocacy

"I become a hurricane" in *Emerge Literary Journal*

"I imagine turning to stare into the face" in *Kissing Dynamite*

"Pseudonymous" in *Eunoia Review*

"How to be a mystery" (published as "Observations during a winter golden hour walk") in *Stirring: A Literary Collection*

"A final supper" (published as "Sonnet With A Final Supper") in *The Orchards Poetry Journal*

"True Story" in *AIOTB: As It Ought to Be Magazine*

"Geo Logic" in *Footprints: an anthology of new ecopoetry* by Broken Sleep Books

"Solastalgia" in *perhappened*

This book would not have been possible without the many good folks who have inspired and supported me throughout the years of writing these poems.

Gratitude to people in the Iowa State Creative Writing & Environment MFA: my professors at Iowa State, especially K. L. Cook, my interdisciplinary mentor, and Deb Marquart, an endless well of encouragement; my classmates, colleagues, and friends who saw many of these poems in their early forms; extra thanks to Bri Stoever, Aimee Burch, Allison Boyd Justus, Richard Frailing, Julia Bilek, Nancy Hayes, Riley Morsman, Kate Wright, Crystal Stone, Renee Christopher, for community in poetry.

An abundance of thanks to the Friends of Lakeside Lab for the generous gift of a writing residency, initially offered in 2020, and then offered again in 2021. Many of the poems here were edited at the picnic tables overlooking Lake Okoboji, after some time in the sun in a kayak.

Forever thankful for friends and family for their constancy to balance out my inconsistency: Tatay, Nanay, Ati, Kuya Lioneil, Kuya LL, Holli, Julie, Amanda. And finally, Aaron: I am eternally grateful to you.

ABOUT THE AUTHOR

Caroliena Cabada writes poetry and fiction. She was the recipient of the 2018-2019 Pearl Hogrefe Fellowship in Creative Writing at Iowa State University, where she earned her MFA in 2021. Her writing has been published in numerous online and print magazines, and was selected for Best Small Fictions 2021. She teaches first-year composition and creative writing at the University of Nebraska-Lincoln, where she is earning her PhD in English with a specialization in Ethnic Studies.

ABOUT THE PRESS

Unsolicited Press is based out of Portland, Oregon and focuses on the works of the unsung and underrepresented. As a womxn-owned, all-volunteer small publisher that doesn't worry about profits as much as championing exceptional literature, we have the privilege of partnering with authors skirting the fringes of the lit world. We've worked with emerging and award-winning authors such as Tara Stillions Whitehead, Heather Lang Cassera, Shann Ray, Amy Shimshon-Santo, Brook Bhagat, Kris Amos, and John W. Bateman.

Learn more at unsolicitedpress.com. Find us on twitter and instagram.

Printed in the USA
CPSIA information can be obtained
at www.ICGtesting.com
JSHW080023230624
65077JS00002B/33

9 781963 115031